THE
GATEWAYS
HAGGADAH

REBECCA REDNER

Editorial Committee
Howard Blas
Rabbi Martin Cohen
Rachel Fadlon
Michele Fried
Lisa Friedman
Nancy Mager
Arlene Remz

Project editor: Terry Kaye
Design: Tabak Design
Illustration: Rebecca Redner
Photography: Jordyn Rozensky

Copyright © 2015 Gateways: Access to Jewish Education
Published by Behrman House, Inc., Springfield, New Jersey
www.behrmanhouse.com
ISBN: 978-0-87441-929-0
Manufactured in the United States of America

CONTENTS

Library of Congress Cataloging-in-Publication Data

Redner, Rebecca, author.
  The gateways Haggadah : a seder for the whole family / [written and illustrated] by Rebecca Redner.
    pages cm
  English and Hebrew.
  ISBN 978-0-87441-929-0
1. Haggadah—Adaptations. 2. Seder. 3. Passover--Prayers and devotions. 4. Jewish families—Prayers and devotions. I. Title.
  BM674.795.R43 2014
  296.4'5371—dc23
                    2014026835

WHAT IS PASSOVER?

How would you feel if you had to work all day without a break? Long ago, the Jews were slaves in Egypt. They had to work every day without any rest.

But God helped the Jews escape from slavery. Passover is the holiday when Jews celebrate being free.

We celebrate Passover with this seder. At the seder we will sing songs, say prayers, and eat holiday foods that help us remember the Passover story.

THE SEDER PLATE

We put a seder plate on the table. The seder plate holds Passover foods. Usually each food's name is written on the seder plate in Hebrew and in English. We learn about the Passover holiday from these foods. Can you figure out where all of the foods on your seder plate go?

The **shank bone** reminds us of how the Jews made a special lamb meal, called a sacrifice, to thank God for their freedom.

Maror and **chazeret** are bitter herbs. The bitter taste of maror and chazeret reminds us of how unhappy and bitter life was for the Jews who were slaves in Egypt.

Charoset is usually a mixture of apples, nuts, honey, wine, and spices. The color and soft texture of charoset reminds us of the mortar the Jewish slaves used long ago in Egypt. Mortar is a kind of cement that is used to help bricks stick together.

The roasted **egg** has a round shape. If you run your finger around an egg you will always come back to the point where you began. The round shape of an egg reminds us that every year we go around the same cycle of months and seasons.

Karpas is a vegetable that grows in the spring. This spring vegetable helps us to think about the new leaves and plants that grow during the time we celebrate Passover.

SETTING THE TABLE

On Passover we put items on the table that we don't use on a regular night. Can you help your mom or dad set the table with these Passover items?

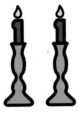

seder plate

Kiddush cup

matzah cover

candles

haggadot

Elijah's cup

bottle of wine or grape juice

bowl of salt water

three pieces of matzah on a plate

Miriam's cup

LIGHTING THE CANDLES

Tonight the holiday of Passover begins. We light candles to celebrate the beginning of Passover.

The light of the candles creates a golden glow. This light makes the house feel cozy and can make us feel good inside. The Passover candles stay lit until they burn down by themselves.

Light the candles.

Carefully wave your hands over the candles three times.

Cover your eyes.

Say the blessings:

בָּרוּךְ אַתָּה יְיָ אֱלֹהֵינוּ מֶלֶךְ הָעוֹלָם
אֲשֶׁר קִדְּשָׁנוּ בְּמִצְוֹתָיו וְצִוָּנוּ
לְהַדְלִיק נֵר שֶׁל [שַׁבָּת וְשֶׁל] יוֹם טוֹב.

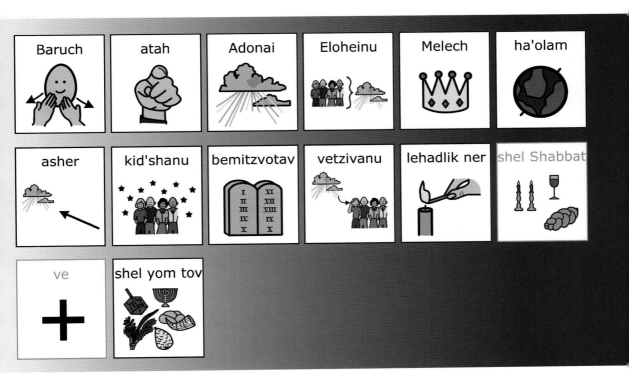

Thank you God, Ruler of the world, who makes us holy
with mitzvot and tells us to light candles on [Shabbat
and on] holidays.

9

LIGHTING THE CANDLES
(continued)

בָּרוּךְ אַתָּה יְיָ אֱלֹהֵינוּ מֶלֶךְ הָעוֹלָם
שֶׁהֶחֱיָנוּ וְקִיְּמָנוּ וְהִגִּיעָנוּ לַזְּמַן הַזֶּה.

| Baruch | atah | Adonai | Eloheinu | Melech | ha'olam |
| sheheche-yanu | vekiyemanu | vehigiyanu | lazman hazeh | | |

Thank you God, Ruler of the world, for giving us life, helping us, and leading us to today.

ORDER OF THE SEDER

Seder means "order" in Hebrew. We call the Passover celebration a seder because we follow a schedule and do everything in a particular order. We begin the seder by reading or singing the seder's schedule. What part of the seder is your favorite?

Kadesh	Urchatz	Karpas	Yachatz	Maggid

Rochtzah	Motzi Matzah	Maror	Korech	Shulchan Orech

Tzafun	Barech	Hallel	Nirtzah

KADESH • DRINKING WINE

We drink wine or grape juice to celebrate Jewish holidays. The sweet taste of these drinks made from grapes makes us feel joyful and ready to celebrate. During the Passover seder we will drink four cups of wine or grape juice! Now it is time to say Kiddush, the blessing over wine and grape juice.

 THE FIRST CUP

Pour wine or grape juice into your Kiddush cup.

Hold your Kiddush cup.

Say the blessings:

בָּרוּךְ אַתָּה יְיָ אֱלֹהֵינוּ מֶלֶךְ הָעוֹלָם
בּוֹרֵא פְּרִי הַגָּפֶן.

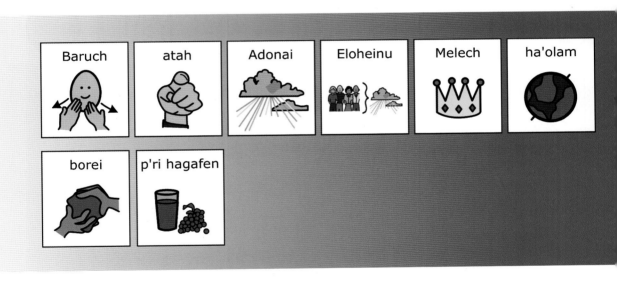

Thank you God, Ruler of the world, who makes the
fruit of the vine (grapes).

(continued)

בָּרוּךְ אַתָּה יְיָ אֱלֹהֵינוּ מֶלֶךְ הָעוֹלָם
שֶׁהֶחֱיָנוּ וְקִיְּמָנוּ וְהִגִּיעָנוּ לַזְּמַן הַזֶּה.

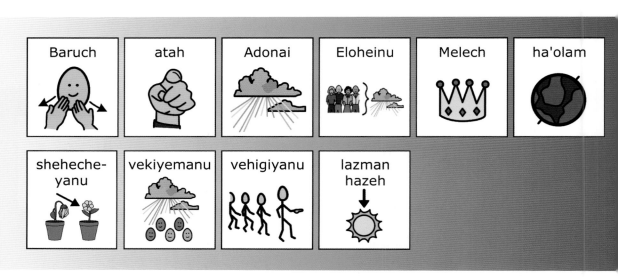

Thank you God, Ruler of the world, for giving us life, helping us, and leading us to today.

Drink your wine or grape juice.*

*If you don't want to drink any wine or grape juice, just put down the Kiddush cup.

URCHATZ • WASHING HANDS

Soon we will eat karpas, the spring vegetable. But first we wash our hands so we will be ready to eat! On Passover, people wash their hands with water from a washing cup instead of using the faucet.

Pour water over both of your hands. Be sure to hold your hands over the sink or a bowl.

Dry your hands.

KARPAS • EATING A VEGETABLE

Spring is a cheerful time of year because the weather gets warmer, and green leaves and vegetables begin to grow. On Passover we eat a spring vegetable to celebrate that spring has come.

Even though we are happy on Passover, we remember the Jews long ago who were sad because they were slaves. We dip our vegetables in salt water to remember the sad, salty tears those Jews cried.

Take one vegetable.

Dip the vegetable in the bowl of salt water.

Say the blessing:

בָּרוּךְ אַתָּה יְיָ אֱלֹהֵינוּ מֶלֶךְ הָעוֹלָם
בּוֹרֵא פְּרִי הָאֲדָמָה.

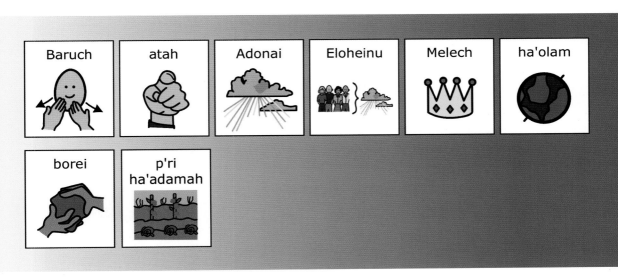

| Baruch | atah | Adonai | Eloheinu | Melech | ha'olam |

| borei | p'ri ha'adamah |

Thank you God, Ruler of the world, who makes fruit of the earth (vegetables).

Eat your vegetable.*

*If you don't want to eat the vegetable, just put it down on your plate.

YACHATZ • BREAKING THE MATZAH

Usually dessert is a sweet treat. But on Passover we also eat an unexpected dessert: a piece of plain matzah called the afikoman. We prepare the afikoman now, and then put it away until the end of the seder. Many families hide the afikoman so the children can have fun searching for it later!

Uncover the matzah.

Take the middle matzah.

Break the middle matzah into two pieces.

Put the smaller piece of matzah back onto the matzah plate.

Put the larger piece of matzah in an afikoman bag or wrap it in a napkin.

Give the afikoman to an adult. The adult will hide the afikoman. Later tonight, during Tzafun, the children will get a chance to find the afikoman.

This adult hid the afikoman under the piano cover. Where do you think the adults in your family might hide the afikoman?

During Maggid we learn about the Passover story. People who already know a lot about Passover review what they know, and often learn something new. We begin by asking how Passover is different from other nights. Usually the youngest child sings the Four Questions. Who will sing the Four Questions at your seder?

MAH NISHTANAH

מַה נִּשְׁתַּנָּה הַלַּיְלָה הַזֶּה מִכָּל הַלֵּילוֹת?
מִכָּל הַלֵּילוֹת?

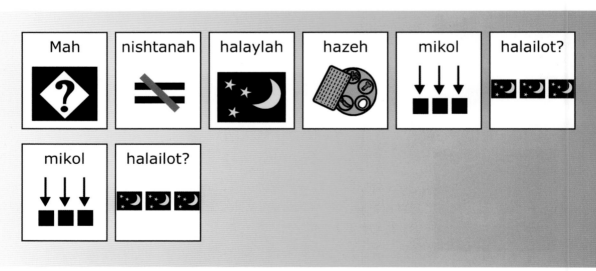

Mah	nishtanah	halaylah	hazeh	mikol	halailot?

mikol	halailot?

Why is Passover night different from all other nights?

שֶׁבְּכָל הַלֵּילוֹת אָנוּ אוֹכְלִין

חָמֵץ וּמַצָּה, חָמֵץ וּמַצָּה,

הַלַּיְלָה הַזֶּה הַלַּיְלָה הַזֶּה, כֻּלוֹ מַצָּה.

הַלַּיְלָה הַזֶּה הַלַּיְלָה הַזֶּה, כֻּלוֹ מַצָּה.

On all other nights we can eat bread or matzah.
But on Passover night we can eat only matzah.

שֶׁבְּכָל הַלֵּילוֹת אָנוּ אוֹכְלִין

שְׁאָר יְרָקוֹת, שְׁאָר יְרָקוֹת,

הַלַּיְלָה הַזֶּה הַלַּיְלָה הַזֶּה, מָרוֹר מָרוֹר.

הַלַּיְלָה הַזֶּה הַלַּיְלָה הַזֶּה, מָרוֹר מָרוֹר.

On all other nights we can eat different kinds of vegetables. But on Passover night we eat bitter herbs.

שֶׁבְּכָל הַלֵּילוֹת אֵין אָנוּ מַטְבִּילִין

אֲפִילוּ פַּעַם אֶחָת, אֲפִילוּ פַּעַם אֶחָת,

הַלַּיְלָה הַזֶּה הַלַּיְלָה הַזֶּה, שְׁתֵּי פְעָמִים.

הַלַּיְלָה הַזֶּה הַלַּיְלָה הַזֶּה, שְׁתֵּי פְעָמִים.

On all other nights, we don't dip our vegetables even once. But on Passover night we dip our vegetables twice.

שֶׁבְּכָל הַלֵּילוֹת אָנוּ אוֹכְלִין

בֵּין יוֹשְׁבִין וּבֵין מְסֻבִּין,

בֵּין יוֹשְׁבִין וּבֵין מְסֻבִּין,

הַלַּיְלָה הַזֶּה הַלַּיְלָה הַזֶּה, כֻּלָּנוּ מְסֻבִּין.

הַלַּיְלָה הַזֶּה הַלַּיְלָה הַזֶּה, כֻּלָּנוּ מְסֻבִּין.

On all other nights, we sit up straight or lean to the side. But on Passover night we lean to the side.

AVADIM HAYINU

This song explains that Passover is different from other days because on Passover we celebrate being freed from slavery.

עֲבָדִים הָיִינוּ, הָיִינוּ. עַתָּה בְּנֵי חוֹרִין, בְּנֵי חוֹרִין.

עֲבָדִים הָיִינוּ, עַתָּה עַתָּה בְּנֵי חוֹרִין.

עֲבָדִים הָיִינוּ, עַתָּה עַתָּה בְּנֵי חוֹרִין, בְּנֵי חוֹרִין.

We were slaves, but now we are free!

Passover is a special occasion, which means it is different from all other nights. Some people enjoy special occasions, but some do not. Now we will read a story about four children who had different feelings about Passover.

THE FOUR CHILDREN

The first child felt excited about Passover! He loved special occasions. He felt so excited that he jumped and flapped and ran.

The excited child's parents taught him to calm his body by doing exercises and then taking deep breaths.

The excited child wanted to know everything about Passover. He asked his parents lots of questions.

The excited child's parents listened to his questions and told him the answers. Then they gave him a book about Passover so he could learn more by himself.

The second child felt upset about Passover. She didn't like special occasions. She liked regular days when she knew what to expect. She yelled and cried and stomped her feet.

The upset child's parents taught her to get past being upset by taking deep breaths, squeezing a ball, or listening to music.

The upset child told her parents that she didn't like Passover. She liked regular days better.

The upset child's parents made her a schedule so she would know what to expect on Passover night. They even gave her time on the schedule to take breaks!

 **The third child** felt confused. He did not recognize the things his family used on Passover.

 The confused child's parents taught him to let them know when he was confused by asking questions like "What's that?" and "Why?"

 Whenever the confused child saw something he did not recognize, he pointed at it and asked for help.

 The confused child's parents helped him practice using Passover objects: a seder plate, matzah, a Kiddush cup, and more. The confused child felt more confident.

 **The fourth child** felt overwhelmed. Passover was full of new routines, foods, and objects. It was too much. She felt excited, upset, and confused all at once.

 The overwhelmed child did not have the words to tell her parents how she felt. She was not able to ask for help.

 The overwhelmed child's parents told her it was okay to feel this way. They said that they would help her feel better.

 The following year, the overwhelmed child's parents began teaching her about Passover many months before Passover began. When Passover finally arrived, it did not feel new and overwhelming.

29

Everybody has different feelings about celebrating occasions like Passover.

How do you feel about celebrating Passover?

Adults know a lot about feelings. Adults can help children manage their feelings and get ready for Passover.

How can caring adults help you?

On Passover we remember the story of how the Jews were freed from slavery in Egypt. The Torah tells us that it is a mitzvah, or a good deed, to talk about this story on Passover.

THE PASSOVER STORY

The Jews were slaves to King Pharaoh in Egypt. They worked hard every day.

A Jewish woman had a baby named Moses. She wanted to hide Moses to protect him from harm.

Carefully, she put Moses in a basket. Then she put the basket to float in the Nile River.

Pharaoh's daughter found the basket in the river. She took Moses and raised him as her son.

Moses grew up and became a shepherd.

One day Moses saw something unexpected: a bush that was on fire but did not burn down.

God's voice came from the bush. God told Moses to go to Egypt and free the Jewish slaves.

Moses went to Egypt and spoke to King Pharaoh. Moses said to Pharaoh, "Let my people go!"

Pharaoh did not want to let the Jews go. Pharaoh said, "No! I will not let them go."

So God sent the Ten Plagues. Plagues were terrible things that hurt the Egyptians.

We are going to pause the Passover story.

 Passover is a joyful holiday, and we show that we are happy by drinking four cups of wine or grape juice.

 But on Passover, we also feel a little sad. Even though the Egyptians made the Jews slaves, it still makes us sad that the Ten Plagues hurt the Egyptians.

 We will show that we feel sad by taking ten drops of wine or grape juice out of our Kiddush cups when we say the names of the Ten Plagues. Taking a little wine or grape juice from our cups shows that we are taking away a little bit of our joy tonight.

 But after that, we can be happy again. Soon we will read the part of the Passover story where the Jews are freed!

Dip your finger or a spoon into your glass of wine.

Touch your finger or spoon to the edge of your plate as you say the name of each plague. Repeat this for each of the ten plagues.

dam	tzfardeiya	kinim	arov	dever
shechin	barad	arbeh	choshech	makat b'chorot

Wipe your finger with a napkin.

The plagues made the Egyptians miserable. They wanted the plagues to stop.

So when Moses went to Pharaoh again and said, "Let my people go!" Pharaoh said "Yes."

The Jews left Egypt quickly, before Pharaoh could change his mind.

There was no time for the Jews to bake bread to eat. They quickly made matzah instead.

When the Jews reached the sea, God made a path through the water. The Jews walked on dry land.

The Jews were free! They thanked God by singing and dancing.

Dayeinu means "it would have been enough." If God had only helped the Jews to leave Egypt, then that would have been enough. But God kept on helping the Jews. God gave the Jews Shabbat, and then the Torah. We are grateful that God gave the Jews so much help.

DAYEINU

אָלוּ הוֹצִיא הוֹצִיאָנוּ, הוֹצִיאָנוּ מִמִּצְרַיִם

הוֹצִיאָנוּ מִמִּצְרַיִם, דַּיֵּינוּ!

דַּי דַּיֵּינוּ, דַּי דַּיֵּינוּ, דַּי דַּיֵּינוּ דַּיֵּינוּ דַּיֵּינוּ!

If God had only taken us out of Egypt, it would have been enough!

36

אִלּוּ נָתַן נָתַן לָנוּ, נָתַן לָנוּ אֶת הַשַׁבָּת
נָתַן לָנוּ אֶת הַשַׁבָּת, דַּיֵּנוּ!
דַּי דַּיֵּנוּ, דַּי דַּיֵּנוּ, דַּי דַּיֵּנוּ דַּיֵּנוּ דַּיֵּנוּ!

If God had only given us Shabbat, it would have
been enough!

אִלּוּ נָתַן נָתַן לָנוּ, נָתַן לָנוּ אֶת הַתּוֹרָה

נָתַן לָנוּ אֶת הַתּוֹרָה, דַּיֵּינוּ!

דַּי דַּיֵּינוּ, דַּי דַּיֵּינוּ, דַּי דַּיֵּינוּ דַּיֵּינוּ דַּיֵּינוּ!

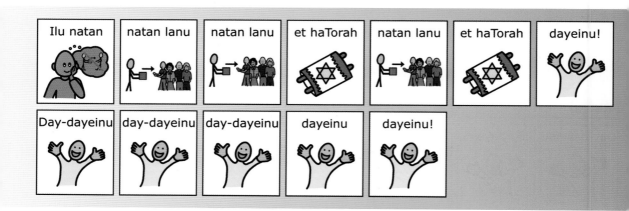

If God had only given us the Torah, it would have been enough!

Three objects on the table tonight help us remember the Passover story. How much of the story can you remember?

The **shank bone** reminds us of the lambs the Jews sacrificed, to thank God for their freedom.

Matzah reminds us that the Jews had to leave Egypt so quickly they had no time to make bread. They quickly baked matzah to bring with them as they left.

The bitter taste of **maror** reminds us of how unhappy and bitter life was for the Jews when they were slaves in Egypt.

THE SECOND CUP

Hold your Kiddush cup filled with wine or grape juice.

Say the blessing:

בָּרוּךְ אַתָּה יְיָ אֱלֹהֵינוּ מֶלֶךְ הָעוֹלָם
בּוֹרֵא פְּרִי הַגָּפֶן.

Baruch	atah	Adonai	Eloheinu	Melech	ha'olam

borei	p'ri hagafen

Thank you God, Ruler of the world, who makes the fruit of the vine (grapes).

Drink your wine or grape juice.*

*If you don't want to drink any wine or grape juice, just put down the Kiddush cup.

ROCHTZAH • WASHING HANDS

We wash our hands again to get ready to eat the Passover meal.
This time, we say a blessing when we wash our hands.

Pour water over both of your hands. Be sure to hold your
hands over the sink or a bowl.

Dry your hands.

Say the blessing:

בָּרוּךְ אַתָּה יְיָ אֱלֹהֵינוּ מֶלֶךְ הָעוֹלָם
אֲשֶׁר קִדְּשָׁנוּ בְּמִצְוֹתָיו וְצִוָּנוּ עַל נְטִילַת יָדָיִם.

Thank you God, Ruler of the world, who makes us holy
with mitzvot and tells us to wash our hands.

MOTZI MATZAH •
EATING THE MATZAH

When the Jews left Egypt they did not have enough time to bake soft and fluffy bread for their long journey in the desert. So they made dough and quickly baked it into a flat bread called matzah. On Passover we eat matzah instead of bread to remember how the Jews long ago ate matzah as they left Egypt.

Take a piece of matzah.

Say the blessings:

בָּרוּךְ אַתָּה יְיָ אֱלֹהֵינוּ מֶלֶךְ הָעוֹלָם
הַמּוֹצִיא לֶחֶם מִן הָאָרֶץ.

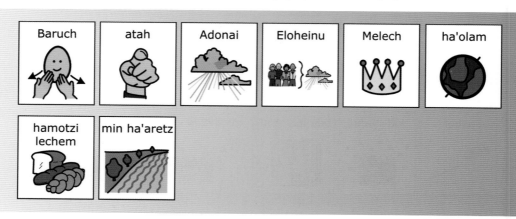

Thank you God, Ruler of the world, who brings bread from the earth.

בָּרוּךְ אַתָּה יְיָ אֱלֹהֵינוּ מֶלֶךְ הָעוֹלָם
אֲשֶׁר קִדְּשָׁנוּ בְּמִצְוֹתָיו וְצִוָּנוּ
עַל אֲכִילַת מַצָּה.

Thank you God, Ruler of the world, who makes us holy
with mitzvot and tells us to eat matzah.

Eat the matzah.*

*If you don't want
to eat any matzah,
put it down on
your plate.

MAROR • EATING A BITTER HERB

Maror is something bitter to eat. We eat bitter herbs to help us remember how sad and bitter life was for the Jewish slaves in Egypt. How do you feel about eating maror?

Take some maror.

Say the blessing:

בָּרוּךְ אַתָּה יְיָ אֱלֹהֵינוּ מֶלֶךְ הָעוֹלָם
אֲשֶׁר קִדְּשָׁנוּ בְּמִצְוֹתָיו וְצִוָּנוּ
עַל אֲכִילַת מָרוֹר.

Baruch	atah	Adonai	Eloheinu	Melech	ha'olam

asher	kid'shanu	bemitzvotav	vetzivanu	al achilat	maror

Thank you God, Ruler of the world, who makes us holy with mitzvot and tells us to eat maror.

Eat the maror.

Maror is very bitter. Some people don't like its taste.*

*If you don't want to try the maror, just leave it on your plate.

KORECH •
EATING A HILLEL SANDWICH

Hillel was a wise man who lived a long time ago. On Passover we eat a sandwich of matzah, maror, and charoset to remember the kind of sandwich Hillel ate.

Take two pieces of matzah and put them on your plate.

Put a little maror and a spoonful of charoset on your plate.

Put the charoset on top of one piece of matzah.

Put the maror on top of the charoset.

Cover the maror and charoset with the second piece of matzah.

Eat the Hillel sandwich.*

*If you don't want to eat the Hillel sandwich, put it down on your plate.

47

SHULCHAN ORECH • EATING DINNER

N̲ow it is time to eat Passover dinner! What is your favorite Passover food?

Before we eat dinner we each put our haggadah away from the table so it does not get dirty.

TZAFUN •
FINDING THE AFIKOMAN

D o you remember when an adult hid the afikoman earlier in the seder? The afikoman must be found before the seder ends! Now the children have the important job of finding the afikoman. Good luck!

Look for the afikoman. Some hiding places may be:

in a plant

under the sofa

in the chair cushions

What other hiding places can you think of?

TZAFUN •
FINDING THE AFIKOMAN *(continued)*

If you find the afikoman,
bring it to an adult.

The adult might give you a small prize!

If you don't find the afikoman, that's okay. Say
"good job" to the person who found the afikoman.

Wait for an adult to give you a piece of the
afikoman. Eat your piece.*

*If you don't
want to eat the
afikoman, put it
down on your
plate.

BARECH • THANKING GOD FOR OUR MEAL

Now that we have finished eating, we say a prayer to thank God for creating the food we eat. We are thankful that we had enough food to eat today.

Say the blessing:

בָּרוּךְ אַתָּה יְיָ הַזָּן אֶת הַכֹּל.

| Baruch | atah | Adonai | hazan | et hakol |

Thank you God for giving food to everybody.

BARECH *(continued)*

THE THIRD CUP

Hold your Kiddush cup filled with wine or grape juice.

Say the blessing:

בָּרוּךְ אַתָּה יְיָ אֱלֹהֵינוּ מֶלֶךְ הָעוֹלָם
בּוֹרֵא פְּרִי הַגָּפֶן.

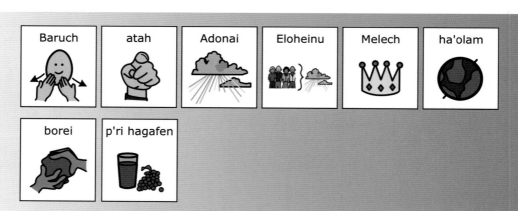

| Baruch | atah | Adonai | Eloheinu | Melech | ha'olam |
| borei | p'ri hagafen | | | | |

Thank you God, Ruler of the world, who makes the fruit of the vine (grapes).

Drink your wine or grape juice.*

*If you don't want to drink any wine or grape juice, just put down the Kiddush cup without drinking.

ELIJAH'S CUP

 On Passover, we imagine that a man named Elijah, or Eliyahu, visits every Jewish house.

 Elijah has his own cup at every seder table. Which cup is Elijah's cup at your table?

 Elijah was a prophet who lived a long time ago in Israel. A prophet is a person who some people believe can speak for God.

 Jewish stories say that one day Elijah will come with the messiah. The messiah is a person who some people believe will bring peace to the world.

 We open the door and imagine Elijah can come in, and we sing a song to Elijah.

ELIYAHU HANAVI

אֵלִיָּהוּ הַנָּבִיא, אֵלִיָּהוּ הַתִּשְׁבִּי,

אֵלִיָּהוּ, אֵלִיָּהוּ, אֵלִיָּהוּ הַגִּלְעָדִי.

בִּמְהֵרָה בְיָמֵינוּ יָבֹא אֵלֵינוּ

עִם מָשִׁיחַ בֶּן דָּוִד, עִם מָשִׁיחַ בֶּן דָּוִד.

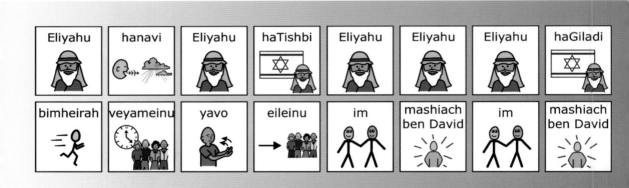

Elijah the prophet, Elijah the man from Tishbi,
Elijah the man from Gilead.

Quickly, he will come to us with the messiah, the son of
King David.

MIRIAM'S CUP

 Some people put a cup filled with water, called Miriam's cup, on the seder table. Miriam was Moses' older sister. She led the Jews in song when they safely crossed the Sea of Reeds.

 It is said that a well full of fresh water followed Miriam in the desert. The Jewish people always had water to drink because of Miriam's well.

 Miriam's cup also makes us think about other strong women like Miriam. Who is a strong woman that you know?

Point to Miriam's cup and say:

זֹאת כּוֹס מִרְיָם, כּוֹס מַיִם חַיִּים.

| Zot | kos | Miryam | kos | mayim chayim |

This is Miriam's cup, the cup of living waters.

HALLEL • SINGING PSALMS

A psalm is a song that praises God. During the Hallel on Passover we sing psalms because we are grateful for everything God did to help the Jews escape from slavery in Egypt. Is there anything else you are grateful for?

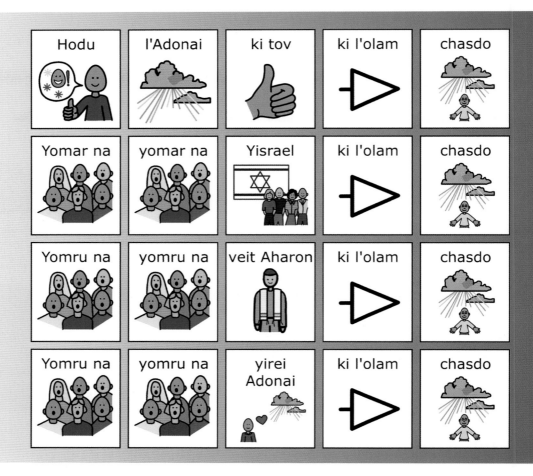

THE FOURTH CUP

Hold your Kiddush cup filled with wine or grape juice.

Say the blessing:

בָּרוּךְ אַתָּה יְיָ אֱלֹהֵינוּ מֶלֶךְ הָעוֹלָם
בּוֹרֵא פְּרִי הַגָּפֶן.

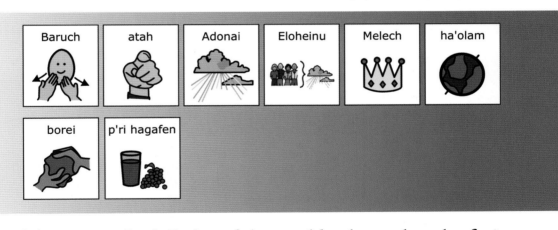

Baruch	atah	Adonai	Eloheinu	Melech	ha'olam
borei	p'ri hagafen				

Thank you God, Ruler of the world, who makes the fruit of the vine (grapes).

Drink your wine or grape juice.*

*If you don't want to drink any wine or grape juice, just put down the Kiddush cup.

NIRTZAH • ENDING THE SEDER

The Passover seder is almost done. We drank four glasses of wine, told the Passover story, ate Passover foods, and sang Passover songs. What was your favorite part of the seder?

Jerusalem is a beautiful city in Israel. We hope that one day we will get to celebrate Passover in Jerusalem!

לְשָׁנָה הַבָּאָה בִּירוּשָׁלָיִם!

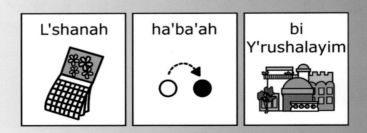

Next year in Jerusalem!

The Passover seder can be so much fun that some people want it to last a little longer. So they sing extra Passover songs. What is your favorite Passover song?

ADIR HU

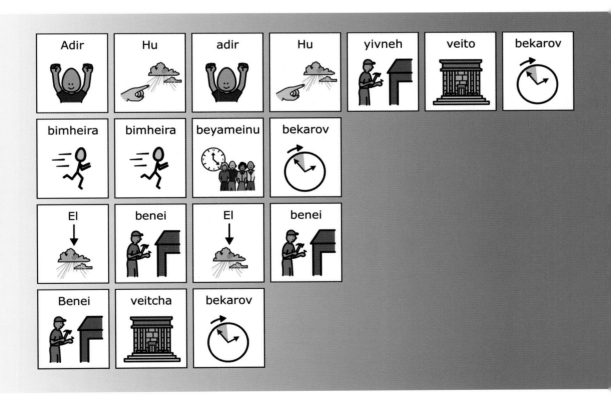

59

CHAD GADYA

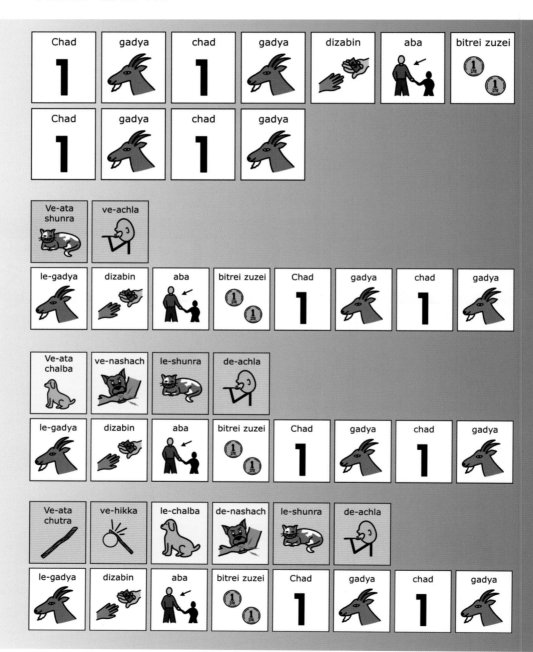

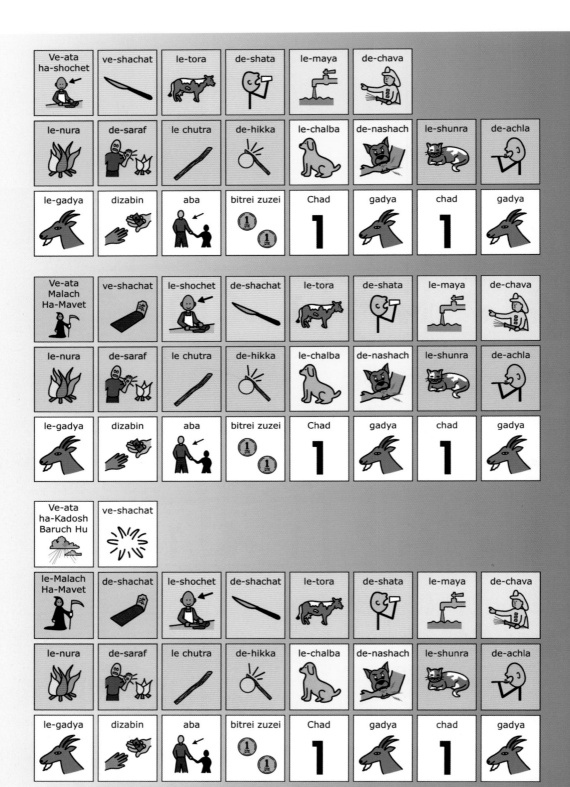

ECHAD MI YODEI'A?

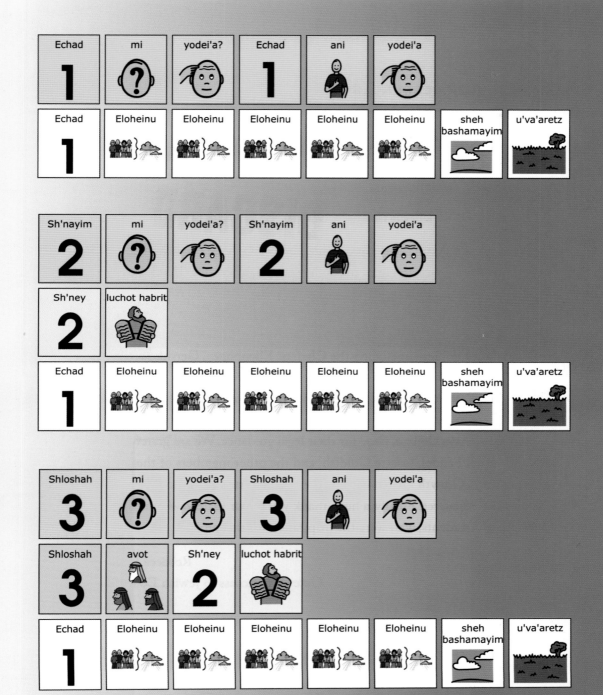

Row 1: Echad **1** | mi | yodei'a? | Echad **1** | ani | yodei'a | Echad **1** | Eloheinu | Eloheinu | Eloheinu | Eloheinu | Eloheinu | sheh bashamayim | u'va'aretz

Row 2: Sh'nayim **2** | mi | yodei'a? | Sh'nayim **2** | ani | yodei'a | Sh'ney **2** | luchot habrit | Echad **1** | Eloheinu | Eloheinu | Eloheinu | Eloheinu | Eloheinu | sheh bashamayim | u'va'aretz

Row 3: Shloshah **3** | mi | yodei'a? | Shloshah **3** | ani | yodei'a | Shloshah **3** | avot | Sh'ney **2** | luchot habrit | Echad **1** | Eloheinu | Eloheinu | Eloheinu | Eloheinu | Eloheinu | sheh bashamayim | u'va'aretz

PASSOVER RESOURCES

For more Passover resources, including the complete seder songs, visit:

www.behrmanhouse.com/passover

www.jgateways.org

ACKNOWLEDGMENTS

Our deepest gratitude to the Chafetz family (Rachel, Larry, Daniel, Tal, and Ben) for helping to make this haggadah possible. Thanks to Jenna Andelman, Rabbi Neal Gold, and Anita Redner z"l for editorial guidance. To Elisa Murphy and her daughter Rachel z"l: you were the inspiration for the Four Children section. We are grateful to the models and their f͏   ͏vitz, Kaplan-W   hoto shoot and   home. We'd like   nstein, Esq. and   ͏l to Micha Gateways   to share r   ͏ay Program

͏Redner ͏cation